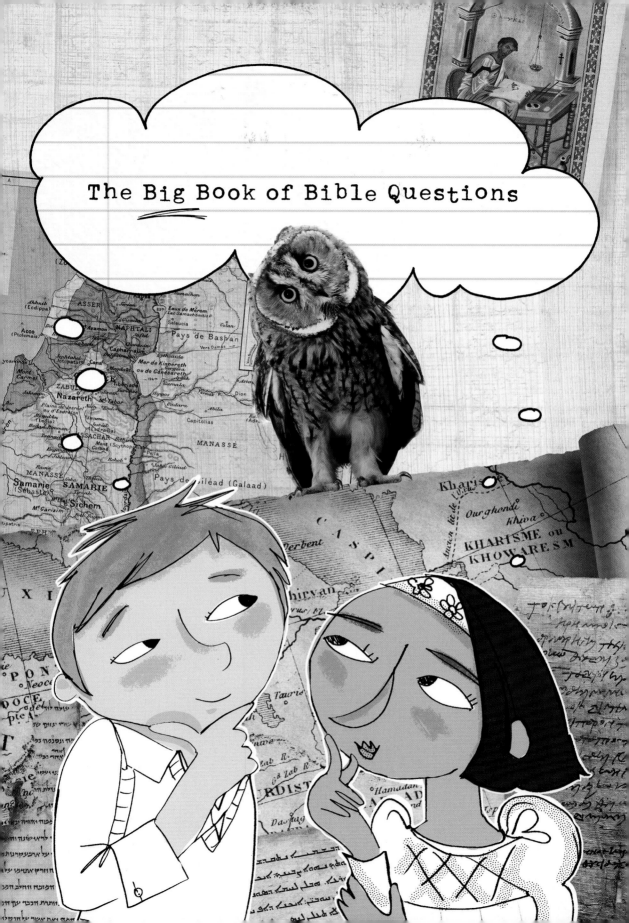

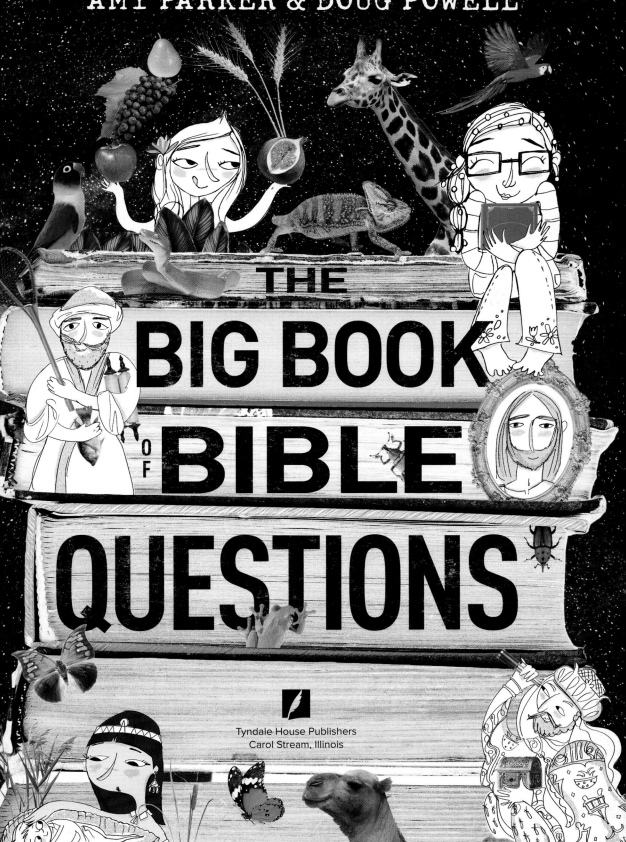

AMY PARKER & DOUG POWELL

THE BIG BOOK OF BIBLE QUESTIONS

Tyndale House Publishers
Carol Stream, Illinois

Contents

New Testament

Dear readers,

We are so excited that *you're* excited to learn more about the Bible. It's a humongous book, written long ago, with many stories and people and places and customs and traditions that may not be familiar to us. All of those things, along with the unfathomable nature of God, can bring up a lot of questions.

In this *Big Book of Bible Questions*, we try to tackle some of those questions, using years of knowledge and experience in exploring those questions ourselves. But this book is not meant to answer every question you have about the Bible—not at all! Our hope is that these questions and answers will be only the beginning of a lifelong love of exploring the Bible and the character of God.

We hope that our answers will give you a deeper understanding of the Bible. But we also know that some answers will only create more questions. And that's okay. When that happens, please dig right in to the text of the Bible itself. And pray for God to reveal his wisdom, to give you understanding. He wants us to know him, and he will be with us every step of the way.

Finally, enjoy this time with your family. Let exploring the Bible together, studying together, and praying together be a regular part of your family time. Encourage each other as you learn more about God and go deeper in your faith. God will bless the investment that you make in your life and in the life of your family.

We're praying for you as you explore *The Big Book of Bible Questions*.

Have fun!

Amy & Doug

Why Do We Have the Bible? Who Wrote It?

Although we are like God in some ways, in many important ways he is completely different from us. God is so different from us, so far beyond our understanding, that we couldn't know anything about him unless he told us. And that is just what he did in the Bible. He told some people about himself, and those people wrote it down for other people—including us!

We often talk about the Bible like it is one book. But really the Bible contains 66 different books! (The Old Testament has 39, and the New Testament has 27.)

The books of the Bible weren't all written at the same time. The oldest part of the Bible was written 1,500 years before the newest part. And the books weren't even all written in the same language. They were written in Hebrew, Greek, and a little bit of Aramaic. And it was written by about forty different people.

Some of these writers were very important people, like kings or people who gave advice to kings. Others were more common people, like fishermen, tax collectors, servants, worship leaders, priests, musicians, tent makers, and soldiers. These people lived in different parts of the world, from as far west as Egypt to as far east as Persia, where Iran is now.

Most of the Old Testament was written by prophets. The books that weren't written by prophets were most likely checked by the prophets to make sure that the written word spoke God's truths.

The New Testament was mostly written by the apostles. Like the prophets, these men were specially chosen by God to speak for him. All of the New Testament was written while at least one of the apostles was still alive.

But the real answer is that *God himself* wrote the Bible. The prophets and the apostles only wrote what God wanted them to say. And God gave them those messages— his messages for his people in the past, and for you and me today.

Who Made God?

No one made God! God has always been alive and always will be alive. Nobody else is like that. He was alive before anything else because he made everything in the whole universe.

Where Is God?

Sometimes people say that God lives in heaven. But really, God is *everywhere*, which is sometimes called *omnipresent*. He is in the deepest cave, he is on the bottom of the ocean, he is farther away than we can see in space, and he is everywhere in between. There is nowhere—anywhere, ever!—that we could go where God is not already there.

5

How Powerful Is God?

God is so powerful that he can do anything—*anything*—he wants to do! There is nothing you can imagine that is so big or so amazing that God could not do it. (Sometimes we use the word *omnipotent*, which means "all-powerful," to say this.) But that doesn't mean God *will* do absolutely anything. There are some things God won't do. That's not because he isn't powerful enough; it's because they are bad things. For example, God will never lie. He has the power to lie, but he is perfectly good, so he never wants to lie. God's goodness keeps him from using his power to do bad things. But his power is so huge that when he wants to do something, he is always able to do it. You know—like create the entire universe just by speaking.

How Smart Is God?

God is *omniscient*, which is another big word meaning that he knows everything there is to know. He knows the name of every animal. He knows the depths of the vastest galaxy. He knows the exact number and color and length of every single hair on your head. He knows it all because *he made it all*.

God knows everything that has ever happened and all the things that will ever happen. And even though the world has been around for a long, long time, he knows everything about how it has changed and how it will change in the future. That's because he decided what the changes would be and when they would happen. There is no question you could ask God that he couldn't answer!

What Does God Look Like?

The Bible says that people were made in the image of God. That makes it sound like God might have eyes and ears and hands just like people do. And sometimes the Bible does talk about how God sees or hears things. Because we need eyes and ears to see and hear, we think of God having eyes and ears too.

But that's not really what "being made in God's image" means. It means we can think about things, make choices, make plans, and judge things, like God can. And it means we can even think about our own thoughts and understand right from wrong, which is why we are responsible for the choices we make.

God can do all these things without a body. How, exactly? Well, we don't really know for sure. God is a spirit, and a spirit is invisible. Still, God knows that is hard for us to understand, so he has appeared in different forms when he wanted to be seen. For example, God spoke to Moses for the first time in the form of a burning bush. But the most important way God made himself appear is when he took the form of a man. The Bible says that Jesus is the invisible God made visible.

What Is a Miracle?

You've probably heard lots of things described as miracles—like an amazing play in a football game or when you finally clean your room. But a miracle isn't just when something unlikely happens. A miracle is when God acts in an unusual way to make something good happen that brings glory to himself.

Sometimes we think of miracles as when God interrupts the way the world works. But that sounds like God is only *sometimes* involved in the world. The Bible says that God makes the world work the way it does and that he is always at work. But sometimes God works in a different way—a way that's uncommon to us—in order to display his power while doing something good.

In the Bible, God uses his miracles to carry out his plans. Often he uses miracles to prove that prophets and apostles have the authority to speak for God. Or God uses his power to save his people, like when he made water flow from a rock in the desert or food fall from the sky.

That's what makes miracles in the Bible different from the supposed miracles in other religions. In the Bible, miracles are God (not a prophet or other person) doing good things for his prophets or for his people. Other religions say they have miracles, but they're not really the same thing. They either don't do good or don't come from God or don't have a purpose at all. True miracles come from God and point us back to his glory.

What Do Angels Look Like?

Angels are part of God's creation, but we can't see them unless God tells them to appear to us. When we can see them, they may look different to different people. Sometimes they look just like average humans, and people don't realize that they are angels. Sometimes they look like men, but their clothes are so white or bright that it is almost blinding. When they don't appear like normal humans, they usually scare the people who see them, and the angel has to tell them not to be afraid, even when he is bringing wonderful news. Even though they sometimes appear as men, that doesn't mean they look like men in heaven.

The Bible talks about two kinds of angels (but there may be more). One kind is called a *cherub*; another is a *seraph*. We see cherubim with a flaming sword guarding Eden after Adam and Eve were sent away. The Ark of the Covenant had two cherubim on the lid, and they are described as having faces and wings. Ezekiel had a vision where he saw hands under cherubim's wings. He also said they had four faces: one of a man, a lion, an eagle, and a cherub. Isaiah had a vision where he saw seraphim, another kind of angel. They seemed to look like men except they had six wings—two covering their faces, two covering their feet, and two to fly. Their voices shook heaven. The apostle John describes many of the same things in the book of Revelation. It may be that this is how angels really look, but it may also be that they are so different from anything we know that this was the best way to describe them so that we could understand.

What Is Faith?

If you asked someone to try to think of other words for *faith*, what do you think the answers would be? You'd probably hear *wishing* or *hoping* or other words like that. But even though people often use *faith* in the same way, that's not what it means in the Bible.

The word that gets translated as *faith* in our Bibles means "firm persuasion and conviction." Have you ever tried to give reasons for something you believe? Faith has to have reasons behind it. Conviction is what you have when there is evidence for what you believe. So biblical faith needs evidence and reasons.

Hebrews 11 gives a great definition of faith: it is the evidence, or the proof, of the things that we can't see (like God and angels and heaven). Then the writer of Hebrews goes on to list a lot of examples of people of faith, along with the amazing things that happened because of faith. (Go read it for yourself!)

Sometimes we hear people say something like, "You just have to have faith." But you can also have faith in something that is not true. It's not enough to "just have faith." You have to have faith in what is true—in what is real—what we have reasons and evidence to believe. And we have plenty of reasons and evidence to believe in God and the Bible.

What Is a Christian?

A Christian is someone who believes that Jesus is the Son of God, sent by God the Father to die for their sins. Christians believe that Jesus paid for their sins when he was crucified on the cross, and that his righteousness—his being perfect in God's eyes—was given to them so that they can be accepted by God. They also believe that on the third day after he died, he was raised from the dead. And they believe salvation is a free gift from God, that there is no way to earn it. All you have to do is believe in Jesus and accept his gift to receive his forgiveness.

Christians who believe all of these things don't have to pay the price for their sins, which is death, because Jesus already paid that price for them. Instead, through the forgiveness of Jesus, they are made holy and righteous and clean. Their sins no longer separate them from God. When their bodies on earth die, that death doesn't last. They will get to live forever with God and Jesus in the heavenly home that he has created for them.

Why Do People Believe Different Things?

After Noah came out of the ark, two kinds of people spread across the earth. One kind believed in God and lived their lives in ways that pleased him. The other group did not believe in God and lived to please themselves.

Today, the people of the world can still be divided this way. But the people who do not believe in God may believe in other things. Some believe in different gods (which don't really exist). Some believe in many gods. Some believe there is no god at all.

Romans 1:20 says, "Ever since the world was created, people have seen the earth and sky. Through everything God made, they can clearly see his invisible qualities—his eternal power and divine nature." Even though God has made himself known to everyone, some people still choose not to believe. Maybe they want to find a way to save themselves. Maybe they do not want God's free offer of salvation. Maybe they want to earn their way into heaven; they want to deserve it. And they're all doing different things to try to please gods that don't exist. It is very sad, but some people will believe in anything but Jesus.

Why Does God Care about People?

God does not need anything but himself. He doesn't need the world, and he doesn't need people. He doesn't need people for company, and he doesn't need them to be his helpers. And yet, he wants us. He loves us.

He wants people to be with him and to know him. But it's not because we are so lovable that he can't resist us. We are all sinners. We disobey God and break his law every day. What we deserve is punishment, every one of us.

So why does God care about people who sin against him? Because *he is love*. God's love is bigger than you could ever imagine. If you piled up all the sins you have ever done and all the ones you will ever do in your whole life, God's love would be bigger. Even if you made a pile of all the sins that have ever been done by everyone who has ever lived and everyone who hasn't even been born yet, God's love would still be bigger than *that*.

That's what makes God's love so powerful, so life changing. He doesn't need to save us, and we certainly don't deserve it. But he does it anyway. Because he is love.

How Did All of Creation Happen in Six Days?

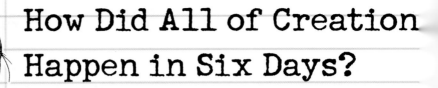

Can you imagine being able to make things happen just by saying them? "I want a chocolate cake." *Boom!* Chocolate cake.

That is what God can do. He is so amazingly powerful that he created everything that exists just by speaking! The Bible tells us that Creation took six days. Some Christians think that means six 24-hour days, and others believe the writer of Genesis was using the word *day* to refer to a longer period of time. But God could have made everything in six seconds if he wanted to. We know for sure that on each day of Creation, God created a certain kind of thing. First, he created light, then the sky the next day, then land and plants the day after that. God used the first three days to make places to put all of the things that he made on the next three days.

On day four God put stars in the sky, as well as the sun and moon. On day five he made the animals in the water and the birds in the air. On day six he made all the land animals. Then God finished his work with his greatest creation: human beings.

The days of Creation tell us that God has a plan and his creation has an order. How long it took is not very important. What is important is believing that God created everything.

Why Did God Put Adam and Eve in the Garden of Eden?

When God created Adam and Eve, they didn't just lie around paradise doing nothing. They had work to do. It was their job to care for the Garden.

Of course, Adam and Eve had all the food they could ever want. But in the middle of all of that beauty and all of those blessings, there was one thing they weren't allowed to do. Just one! And that was to eat from the tree of the knowledge of good and evil. Even though the Bible doesn't say exactly why God put Adam and Eve in the Garden, it looks sort of like a test, doesn't it?

They didn't *need* to eat from that tree, because God had given them a whole Garden of different trees and plants to feed them. But by putting this tree in the Garden and giving them this *one* rule to follow, God may have been seeing if they would obey him. Did they love God enough, trust him enough, to obey?

God, who knows everything, knew that Adam and Eve would fail. And long before they disobeyed him—even before the world was created—God planned to send his Son to save people from their disobedience. Although what Adam and Eve did was wrong, God used their sin to show us how incredibly much he loves us. If Adam and Eve had never been put in that Garden, we wouldn't know how loving or holy God is— or how much we need him.

26

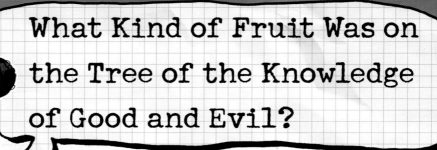

What Kind of Fruit Was on the Tree of the Knowledge of Good and Evil?

Have you ever seen a picture of Adam and Eve disobeying God in the Garden of Eden? What kind of fruit was Eve holding? Most people picture an apple—and even some teachers in Jesus' time thought that's what it was too.

But not everyone thinks the fruit was an apple. Some teachers in Jesus' time thought it was a grape. Others thought it was a fig, which would explain why God made Adam and Eve's first clothes from a fig tree. And yet other teachers at the time of Jesus thought it was not fruit at all, but wheat!

The reason people have pictured so many different foods is because the Bible does not say what kind of food it was. It may be a common food we eat every day that came from that special tree set aside by God. Or it could be a food that we've never even seen or heard of because there was only *one* tree of the knowledge of good and evil. And no one—except God—really knows where that tree is now.

Where Is the Garden of Eden?

The Bible says the Garden was where a river from Eden split into four other rivers: the Pishon, the Gihon, the Tigris, and the Euphrates (see Genesis 2:10-14). There are two rivers named the Tigris and Euphrates that still exist in Turkey, Syria, and Iraq. They connect near the Persian Gulf. If we could follow the rivers upstream to find Eden, it would put the Garden in eastern Turkey. But the Tigris and Euphrates don't start at the same place anymore.

Another problem is that there are no rivers named the Pishon and Gihon anymore. Some people think the Pishon might be the Nile in Egypt and the Gihon could be in Ethiopia, but neither of those rivers is anywhere close to the Tigris and Euphrates.

Different Jewish and Christian teachers have tried to say the missing rivers are underground or that they changed course after the flood of Noah. But no one really knows what happened to them. Plus, the Bible tells us that God stationed cherubim and a flaming sword to guard the entrance of the Garden of Eden. So we probably couldn't find it, even if we tried.

Why Did Noah Build the Ark?

Noah built the ark because God told him to. God saw that the people on earth had become evil. They did so many bad things that God decided to wash the whole world with a Flood that killed all the evil people. Only Noah lived in a way that pleased God. So God told Noah to build an ark—a big boat—where he and his family and all the animals would be safe during the Flood.

How Big Was It?

God told Noah to make the ark 300 *cubits*, or forearms, long. Forearms are usually about 18 inches long (like an adult's forearm!), so the ark was about 450 feet long—that's one and a half football fields! It was 75 feet wide and 45 feet tall, which is about as tall as a four-story building.

How Did He Build It?

God told Noah exactly how to build the ark. He told Noah what kind of wood to use, how to make it waterproof, and exactly how big it needed to be. He even told him where to put the door, how low the roof should be, and how many levels to build inside for the animals. Noah may have built it all by himself, or his three sons may have helped him. The Bible doesn't say how long it took Noah to build the ark, but it probably took years and years.

Where Did Noah's Ark Land?

The Bible says that when the waters from the great Flood sent by God began to drop, the ark landed on a mountain. Even though most people today think it was called Ararat, that's not what the Bible actually says. It says the ark rested on "the mountains of Ararat" (Genesis 8:4). That may not sound like a big difference, but actually it changes the location of where the ark may have touched down.

There is a famous mountain in northeast Turkey called Ararat, and this is the place where most people think the ark landed. But that mountain wasn't called Ararat until Christian times, when Europeans gave it that name. The people who live in the area don't call it Ararat at all. They call it Massis or Agri-Dagh.

Another problem is that the modern-day Ararat is a single mountain rising from the plain, not a group of mountains, as the Bible says. Two hundred miles southwest of Agri-Dagh, there is a chain of mountains called the mountains of Ararat. Local traditions in the villages near there say a mountain called Cudi Dagh or Mount Judi is where Noah landed. For a time, there was even a monastery built on the spot where the ark supposedly rested.

Many people have tried to find the ark over the years, but no one has ever found it. (At least no one has been able to really prove that they found it.)

Why Did God Put a Rainbow in the Sky?

After the Flood was over, Noah and his family worshiped God and thanked him for saving them. God responded by making a promise to Noah, his family, and everyone who would be born after them. God promised that he would never again send a flood to destroy the earth. And although the promise was made to Noah and his descendants, it was also for every living creature. As a sign of this promise, God put a rainbow in the clouds. When you see a rainbow even today, you know that it is there because God is keeping his promise.

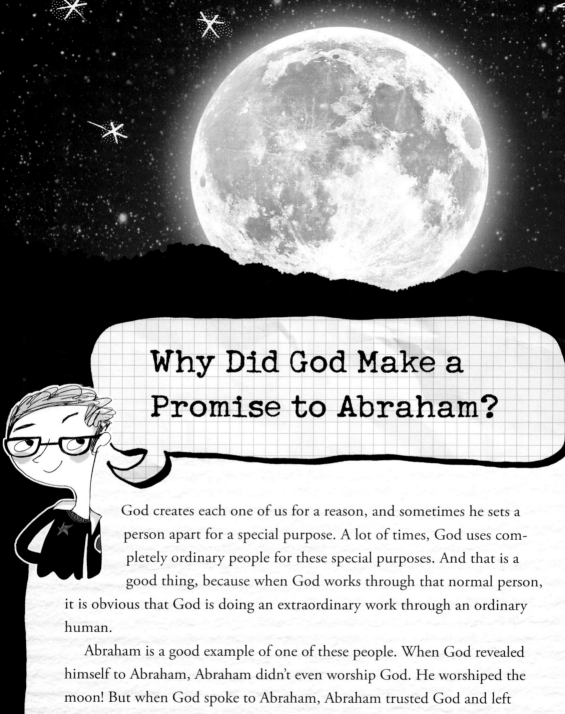

Why Did God Make a Promise to Abraham?

God creates each one of us for a reason, and sometimes he sets a person apart for a special purpose. A lot of times, God uses completely ordinary people for these special purposes. And that is a good thing, because when God works through that normal person, it is obvious that God is doing an extraordinary work through an ordinary human.

Abraham is a good example of one of these people. When God revealed himself to Abraham, Abraham didn't even worship God. He worshiped the moon! But when God spoke to Abraham, Abraham trusted God and left his home. God promised Abraham he would be the father of many nations, which means he would have more children and grandchildren and great-grandchildren than the stars he could see in the sky!

From a human point of view, there was a major problem with this plan. Abraham's wife, Sarah, had never been able to have babies. And when God made this promise to Abraham, she was way past the age of being able to have babies. She should have been a great-great-grandmother by then!

God already knew that, of course. It may have even been one of the reasons that God chose Abraham for his special purpose. How amazing would it be for a woman who had never been able to have babies to give birth to a child in her old age—and then go on to have more descendants than stars in the sky?!

And that is just what happened. Abraham believed God, and Sarah became pregnant with a son. Abraham wasn't perfect, but he did trust God to keep his promises. And God—as always—was faithful. Millions of people alive today—more than all the stars we can see in the sky—are proof that God kept his promise to Abraham.

Why Were Joseph's Brothers So Mean to Him?

Joseph's brothers were really jealous of Joseph. He was one of the youngest brothers, and his mother had died, so he was really close to his father. Joseph's father gave a colorful robe only to Joseph so that he even *looked* more special than the others.

It's normal to be a little jealous of our brothers and sisters sometimes. But Joseph's brothers became so jealous that they sold him to some traders headed for Egypt! Those traders sold him to a ruler, Potiphar, and he liked Joseph a lot. But then Joseph was put in prison for something he didn't do. While he was there, he met another prisoner who was later released and went back to work for the king of Egypt, called Pharaoh. The man told Pharaoh about Joseph, and then Joseph started to work for Pharaoh too. He was so smart and helpful to Pharaoh that he became the highest ruler in Egypt except for Pharaoh.

Joseph's wisdom saved millions of lives in and around Egypt during a long famine—including his own family, who eventually came to ask for help. They didn't recognize Joseph at first, because they never expected their little brother to be the leader of Egypt. But Joseph knew who they were. And Joseph forgave them.

Joseph told his brothers that even though, because of their jealousy, they had meant to hurt him, God used what they had done to do something good. It turns out that if Joseph's brothers hadn't been jealous, millions of people would have starved years later. God is so powerful that he can use bad things to make good things happen.

Why Did Moses' Mom Put Him in the River?

After Joseph brought his family to Egypt, they had lots of children, and then those children grew up and had even more children. There were so many of them that the Egyptians were afraid the descendants of Joseph (called Hebrews) would take over Egypt. So to keep themselves safe, the Egyptians made the Hebrews slaves. But still the Egyptian rulers were afraid the Hebrews would grow too strong. So Pharaoh made a law that all Hebrew boy babies should be killed at birth. Moses' mom just couldn't do that. Instead, she hid him as long as she could. But after a few months she couldn't hide him anymore. So she made a little basket-boat, put baby Moses inside, and let the Nile River carry him away. That way, she thought, Moses would at least have a chance.

And she was right. Pharaoh's daughter found the little baby while she was bathing in the river. She immediately knew that he must have been one of the Hebrew babies, but even so she took him home to live in the palace with her.

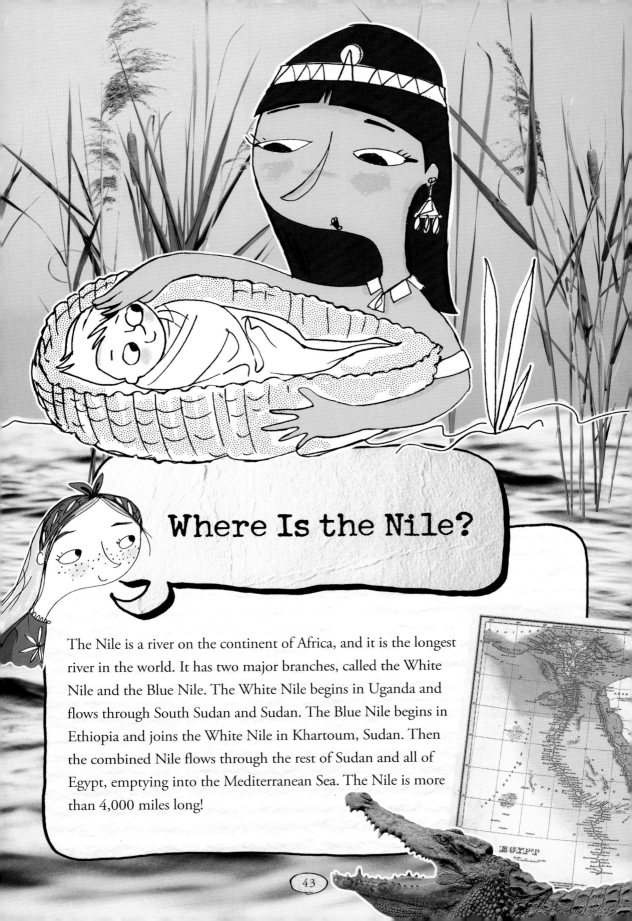

Where Is the Nile?

The Nile is a river on the continent of Africa, and it is the longest river in the world. It has two major branches, called the White Nile and the Blue Nile. The White Nile begins in Uganda and flows through South Sudan and Sudan. The Blue Nile begins in Ethiopia and joins the White Nile in Khartoum, Sudan. Then the combined Nile flows through the rest of Sudan and all of Egypt, emptying into the Mediterranean Sea. The Nile is more than 4,000 miles long!

Why Didn't Pharaoh Recognize Moses?

When Moses stood before Pharaoh to demand that the Hebrews be released, he had been gone from Egypt for forty years. You'd think that Pharaoh would have been glad to see him, or at least would have asked where he had been and what he'd been doing all that time. But Pharaoh didn't even seem to know who Moses was.

No one knows for sure why this is, but the best place to look for an answer is eighty years earlier, when Pharaoh's daughter pulled baby Moses from the river and adopted him as her son. Have you ever wondered why she did that? It could be that baby Moses was super cute and Pharaoh's daughter couldn't resist him. The Bible does tell us that she felt sorry for him. But it's probably really because Pharaoh had no son to take his place.

After Moses was adopted, he would have been raised to become the next ruler of Egypt. But instead, Moses ran from Egypt and became a shepherd in Midian, far away. During the time he was gone, Pharaoh died, and probably because he didn't have a son to take his place, someone from a different family became the ruler. That person may not have known who Moses was. Then that new Pharaoh may have died and left the throne to his own son, who almost definitely wouldn't have known Moses.

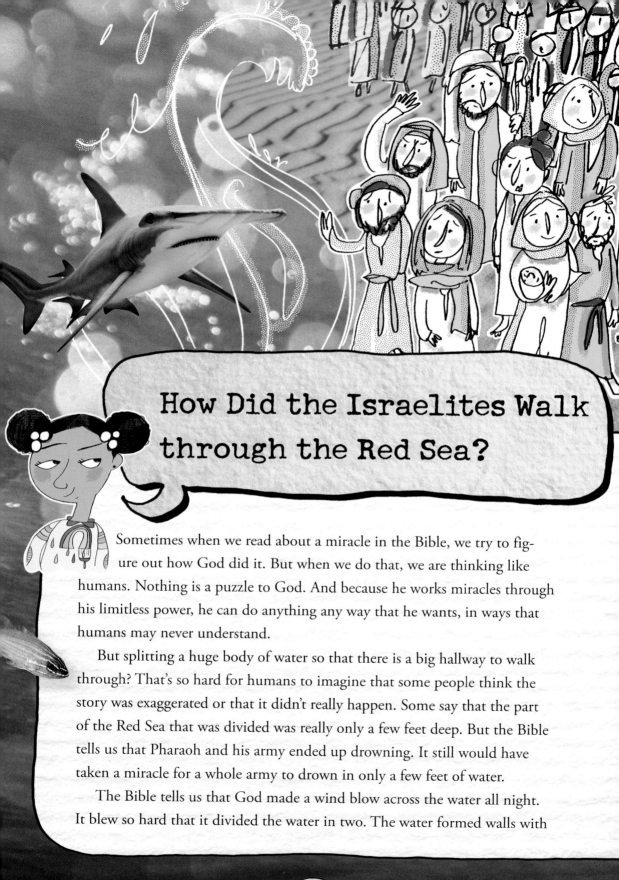

How Did the Israelites Walk through the Red Sea?

Sometimes when we read about a miracle in the Bible, we try to figure out how God did it. But when we do that, we are thinking like humans. Nothing is a puzzle to God. And because he works miracles through his limitless power, he can do anything any way that he wants, in ways that humans may never understand.

But splitting a huge body of water so that there is a big hallway to walk through? That's so hard for humans to imagine that some people think the story was exaggerated or that it didn't really happen. Some say that the part of the Red Sea that was divided was really only a few feet deep. But the Bible tells us that Pharaoh and his army ended up drowning. It still would have taken a miracle for a whole army to drown in only a few feet of water.

The Bible tells us that God made a wind blow across the water all night. It blew so hard that it divided the water in two. The water formed walls with

dry land in between them. After the Hebrews had crossed, God stopped the wind, and the water fell back into place, covering the army that was chasing the Hebrews.

How God made it happen is not as important as knowing that God *did* make it happen. That miracle freed the Hebrews—the Israelites—from slavery and showed them that they were God's chosen people. Of course, God didn't have to split the Red Sea. He could have sent flaming chariots to fly the Israelites over the water. He could have made them disappear on one side and reappear on the other. But what God did caused his people to walk through the middle of a sea, on dry land, with only the wind holding up the surrounding walls of water. This gave God's people plenty of time to marvel at his astounding power. It surely made them grateful to be called his people!

What's the Difference between Noah's Ark and the Ark of the Covenant?

Sometimes, words can have more than one meaning. It can be confusing, especially when it's an odd word like *ark*, and especially when the two meanings are so different, and *especially* when the two words appear in the same big book . . . like the Bible.

Ark, when it's used to describe Noah's ark, is just another word for boat—

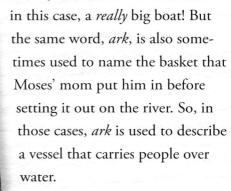

in this case, a *really* big boat! But the same word, *ark*, is also sometimes used to name the basket that Moses' mom put him in before setting it out on the river. So, in those cases, *ark* is used to describe a vessel that carries people over water.

The Ark of the Covenant, however, is a very different object. It's a super-special storage chest that held the Ten Commandments, the stone tablets that God himself wrote on! It was about the size of a box where you might keep toys or Christmas decorations. But this box was covered completely with gold, inside and out. It had rods running down each side to carry it with, and only the priests could carry it. When they did carry it, they covered it with special cloths. It was kept in the holiest section in the Tabernacle.

How Tall Was Goliath?

What do you think it looked like when David stood in front of Goliath? Goliath towered over him, right? But exactly how tall was he?

Some versions of the Bible say that Goliath was over nine feet tall—except there was no such thing as *feet* when the Bible was written. Other versions say that he was six cubits and a span, which sounds funny since we don't really use cubits to measure things anymore. But a cubit is about eighteen inches, and a span is half that (about nine inches), so that means Goliath would have been almost ten feet tall. There are some Bibles that say he was almost seven feet tall, or four cubits and a span. That's because some of the oldest copies of 1 Samuel (they existed before Jesus was born!) use this number.

No matter how you look at it, though, Goliath was a giant. Even if he

was only six foot nine, he still would have been a giant compared to other people back then. At six foot nine, Goliath would be two inches taller than the average professional basketball player and seven inches taller than the average professional football player! Either way, it would take a brave kid, strong in the power of God, to stand up to a giant like that.

7'
6'8"
6'6"
6'4"
6'2"
6'
5'8"
5'6"
5'4"
5'2"
5'
4'8"
4'6"
4'4"
4'2"

How Old Was David?

Although David is usually pictured as a young boy, the Bible doesn't really say how old he was when he fought Goliath. What it does say is that David had seven older brothers. Three of them were in the army with King Saul. We know that men twenty years old and older were old enough to be soldiers back then. And if only three of David's brothers were twenty or older, then four of them were younger than twenty. That means David could not have been older than about fifteen. But just because a man was twenty, that didn't mean that he *was* a soldier, just that he *could* be.

What we know for sure is that Saul thought David was too young for battle. There are other clues about his age in the stories about Saul, Samuel, and David, but in the end we just don't know for sure. He could have been as young as thirteen or as old as nineteen. More importantly, though, we know that David could not defeat Goliath on his own. David depended on God's strength, and God's glory was revealed in David's weakness.

How Did He Beat Goliath?

David used only a sling and a stone. He whipped the sling around and around and let go at just the perfect time, sending the stone straight for Goliath's head. He probably had a lot of practice using the sling to protect his father's sheep, but it seems unlikely that he only needed one stone to take down a giant warrior like Goliath. And that's where God came in. When the Philistines saw that their strongest warrior had been defeated, they took off running, and the Israelite army chased after them.

Why Did God Make Solomon So Smart?

When Solomon became king, God appeared to him in a dream and asked him what he wanted. God told Solomon to simply ask for whatever he wanted, and God would give it to him. Solomon could have asked God for *anything*!

First, Solomon praised God for blessing his father, David. Then he admitted that, now that he was king, he didn't really know how to be a good king like his father was. And it was a lot of pressure to be the king of God's own people—too many people to count! Solomon told God that what he needed most to be a good king was wisdom, so that he could make good decisions for God's people. God was pleased with Solomon's request. And he told Solomon that because he'd asked for wisdom—a gift that helped others rather than being selfish—his request would be granted.

And boy, was it granted! Solomon became known all over the world for his great wisdom. He was not only a wise judge, but he taught people about other things, like plants and animals. He wrote proverbs and songs. Kings from all over would send their men to Solomon just to learn from his wisdom.

To top it off, God also gave Solomon the gifts he *didn't* ask for. He gave Solomon fame and riches and a long, peaceful life.

Why Did God Choose Esther to Save His People?

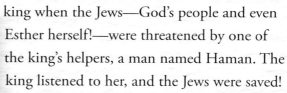

God often chooses to work through people. But it's not necessarily because they're special or they earned it, and it is not because God needs help. A lot of times, God chooses a person who looks like the *least* likely person on the planet that God could use.

Esther was an orphaned Jewish girl who lived in Susa (a city in modern-day Iran). Some Jews still lived there after being captured and taken to Babylonia. Esther had been adopted by her cousin, Mordecai, who took care of her like his own daughter.

But God had given Esther the gift of beauty. And when the king was looking for a new wife, he thought she was the most beautiful woman in the kingdom and made her queen. As queen, Esther was able to speak to the king when the Jews—God's people and even Esther herself!—were threatened by one of the king's helpers, a man named Haman. The king listened to her, and the Jews were saved!

God didn't *have* to use Esther to save his people. Even Mordecai had told Esther that if she didn't do it, God would send someone else! But Mordecai also reminded Esther that maybe she was chosen to be queen for that very reason. And because Esther was brave enough to accept the challenge, she became a part of the story of God's people. Through Esther's story, we can see that God can use us, even the most unlikely of us, to help bring good things to his people.

Why Did Haman Want to Hurt God's People?

Except for the king, Haman was the most powerful person in the land. This power made him think he was better than all the other people. He was so powerful that everyone who saw him bowed to him, just as they did to the king—well, everyone but Esther's cousin, Mordecai.

The Bible never says why Mordecai would not bow to Haman. It may be because Haman was an Amalekite, one of the enemies of the Jews. But we do know that when Haman found out that Mordecai wouldn't bow, he also found out that Mordecai was a Jew. And instead of punishing only Mordecai, he decided to try to have all the Jews in the kingdom killed.

But in the end, we were reminded that God is in control over all things. God took Haman's evil plan and used it to reveal his own power, goodness, and faithfulness to his people.

What Are the Psalms?

Have you ever looked at the book of Psalms and wondered why it looks different from most of the other books in the Bible? The lines are shorter, and they kind of look like the words to a song. That's because *they are*!

It might be hard to see at first because there's no music to read, and we are used to words in a song rhyming and having the same rhythm. But remember, we are reading English words that were translated from Hebrew. The words that rhyme in Hebrew may not rhyme in English. If you'll look closely, though, you will see directions or descriptions for the song leaders at the beginning of some of the psalms.

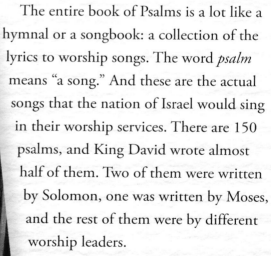

The entire book of Psalms is a lot like a hymnal or a songbook: a collection of the lyrics to worship songs. The word *psalm* means "a song." And these are the actual songs that the nation of Israel would sing in their worship services. There are 150 psalms, and King David wrote almost half of them. Two of them were written by Solomon, one was written by Moses, and the rest of them were by different worship leaders.

Open one up and try to sing it yourself!

What Is a Proverb?

A proverb is a saying that teaches something true about life in a way that is easy to remember. The proverbs teach about knowing right from wrong. They also teach about how to live your life wisely and make good decisions.

Who Wrote Proverbs?

There were several people who wrote the proverbs that are in the Bible. The writer who wrote the most was King Solomon. This makes sense, of course, because God had given him great wisdom. But he wasn't the only wise man at the time. At least four other authors wrote parts of Proverbs, but we don't know very much about them. Two of them were called Agur and Lemuel. The only other writers were called the "men of Hezekiah," who copied down the proverbs of Solomon. But remember, as with all of the books of the Bible, it's not about the men who wrote them—it's about God, who gave them the message to write.

Final answer? God. Just like the rest of the Bible, God is the true author of Proverbs.

Why Did Isaiah Tell about the Birth of Jesus?

If some random person told you that he was the Son of God, the Savior of the world, would you believe it? I hope not! Anybody could *say* that they were the Son of God. But what would it take for you to believe them?

After Adam and Eve sinned, God promised to send a Savior to the world. And as time went on, different prophets described that Savior in different ways. God told each of the prophets something different about the Messiah that no one else knew.

All of that information put together formed a description of a very specific person. The prophets told where he would be from, how he would be born, how he would die, and many other specific details about this one person, this Savior. God did it this way so that the people would recognize him, so that they would know when the true savior had come. Only one person could be all of the things that God had revealed. And that person was Jesus.

So, when God told Isaiah some of the clues about who this Savior would be, Isaiah wrote them down and shared them with God's people.

Why Did Daniel Get Thrown into a Lions' Den?

Daniel was an important helper to King Darius in Persia. The kingdom was so big that Darius had lots of helpers, but Daniel was the most helpful of them all. He was so helpful that the king planned to put him in control of the entire kingdom. This made some of the other helpers jealous, so they came up with a plan to get rid of Daniel.

The jealous helpers knew that Daniel was a Jew who believed in God. So they convinced the king to make a law saying that everyone had to pray to the king and *only* the king for thirty days. Anyone who didn't would be thrown in a den where lions were kept. Sure enough, even when Daniel heard about the law, he wouldn't pray to the king. He only prayed to God.

As soon as they saw Daniel break the law, Daniel's enemies told the king. The king was very sad because he didn't want to hurt someone who was so helpful to him. But he had made the law, and he had to follow it. So he had Daniel thrown into the lions' den, hoping that Daniel's God would rescue him.

The next morning the king discovered that Daniel's God did in fact rescue him! Then the king made a new law: a law that said that everyone should worship the God of Daniel. Once again, God took something meant to be a bad thing and turned it into a very good thing. If Daniel hadn't been thrown into the lions' den, the people of the kingdom would not have worshiped the one true God.

How Many Lions Were in the Den? Where Was It?

When Nebuchadnezzar conquered Judah, Daniel was one of the Jews who was captured and taken to Babylon, which is in the modern country of Iraq. But even though he was a prisoner, Daniel was raised up by God to become an adviser to four different kings. And even though each king tested Daniel's faith, he never lost his trust in God.

The ruins of Babylon can still be seen to this day about fifty miles south of Baghdad. The lions' den would probably have been somewhere around there. At that time and place, as mean as it sounds, it was not unusual for a criminal to be put to death by being fed to lions.

The Bible doesn't say how many lions there were. However, there is an ancient Jewish book that also tells the story of Daniel in the lions' den, and it says there were seven lions. Other details from that book don't match up with the book of Daniel, so that number may not be correct. But whether it was two lions or ten, one thing is for sure: God kept Daniel safe from every single one of them.

Why Did a Fish Swallow Jonah?

When God told Jonah to go to Nineveh and tell the people to stop sinning against God, Jonah did not want to go. In fact, he tried to run away from God! He got on a boat heading in the opposite direction from Nineveh.

While Jonah was traveling, a dangerous storm began, and it looked like the ship would be destroyed. Jonah told the other people on the ship that it was storming because he had disobeyed God. He told the other men to

throw him into the ocean to calm the storm and save themselves. So they picked him up and threw him into the ocean.

While Jonah was in the water, God sent a huge fish to swallow him. Jonah stayed in the fish for three days, which was enough time for him to repent of his sins and promise to obey God. Then the fish spat Jonah up, right onto the shore. And you'd better believe that Jonah headed straight for Nineveh. God used a big storm and a big fish to change Jonah's heart.

Why Were There Prophets? Who Were They?

If you got a letter in the mail saying that it was a special message from God, would you believe it? Probably not! Of course, God knows that. He knew that people would need some way of testing whether or not the prophets that he sent were real. And he knew that the prophets would have to do something pretty amazing to get people to listen.

So God gave his prophets miracles to perform. Miracles not only got the attention of the people who saw them, but they were also proof that the prophet who did the miracle spoke the very words of God. For instance, God told Moses to use his staff as a sign. When Moses threw his staff on the ground, it would turn into a snake. When he picked it up again, it would turn back into a staff.

Prophets also told at least one thing that would happen in the future during their lifetime. When it came true, the people would know that the prophet was really from God. Also, a prophet could never be wrong. If a prophet ever told something that didn't come true, people would not only stop believing him or her, but they also believed that the prophet should be put to death! Moses was the first prophet to write God's messages down. For the next thousand years, there was always a prophet in the land proclaiming God's messages to his people. Malachi was the last prophet of the Old Testament.

Why Did an Angel Visit Mary and Joseph?

God had an important message to deliver to Mary and Joseph—maybe the most important message of all time. And he knew that this message was going to be a bit hard to believe. He couldn't use just anyone to deliver it. So he sent an angel named Gabriel to tell Mary and Joseph that they would be parents to the Savior of the world, God's own Son.

Even with an angel as the messenger, that news was a bit difficult to understand. Mary was a young, unmarried girl, engaged to marry Joseph. How could she have a baby now? And what would Joseph think when he found out that the girl he was going to marry was already going to have a baby?

But Gabriel explained everything. He told Mary that the Holy Spirit would cause her to become pregnant. He told Joseph that Mary's baby was the Savior God had promised through the prophets. And even though they had no idea what lay ahead, both Mary and Joseph agreed to be a part of the plan—the best plan ever—God's plan to save the world.

Why Did Jesus Come to Earth?

God is perfect in every way. And one of the ways he shows his perfection is by giving us his law so that we know how to act toward him and toward other people. This law is in the Ten Commandments, but it is also written in your conscience: that part of you that helps you know right from wrong.

No one can be with God unless they keep his law perfectly. But we are sinners, and we break his law all the time. So how can we be with God? We can't fix our own sin. We can say we are sorry and try to change, but that doesn't pay for the sin we already

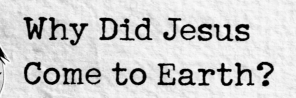

did. And God can't just ignore our sins and forgive us, because that would let sin go unpunished—which is a bad thing. And God cannot do bad things. Of course, our perfect God knows all of this, so he came up with a perfect solution.

Even though we are helpless in our sin, God loves us so much that he sent his own Son, Jesus, to earth to live as a man. Jesus never sinned, not even once in his whole life. He was the only person who ever lived that kept God's law perfectly. So when Jesus was crucified, he wasn't punished for his sins. He was punished for your sins. And mine. And those of everyone who would ever believe in him.

Jesus paid for our sins with his perfect obedience. And his perfection was given to us. Once you accept this gift of grace, when God looks at you, he only sees the perfection of Jesus. That's what it means to be forgiven by him. Even more amazing, God's forgiveness is free. You can't earn it. You can't buy it. You only have to believe in Jesus, your Savior, God's only Son.

Why Did Angels Appear When Jesus Was Born?

When Jesus was born, angels announced his birth, the birth of the Savior that God had promised through the prophets for over a thousand years. It was an announcement to the whole world, really, but the angels chose to deliver it in person to some shepherds in a field.

In those days, people didn't really like shepherds and looked down on them. By appearing to them, the angels were showing that God came to save all kinds of people, even people that may be looked down on or disliked. This also showed that Jesus wouldn't be any regular king. He would be the King

of kings, and yet a humble servant-king to even the humblest of people.

The angels may have also come as another reminder to Mary and Joseph that Jesus truly was the Son of God. Even though this little baby boy looked absolutely normal in every way, angels came down from heaven and announced his birth. And the shepherds went to Mary and Joseph and told them about it. The shepherds gave Mary and Joseph yet another reason to believe what Gabriel had told them months before, maybe at a time when they needed to hear it most.

Who Were the Wise Men? Where Did They Come From?

When you picture the wise men, how many do you see? Three, right? But the Bible doesn't actually say how many there were. We probably picture three because of the three gifts they brought: gold, frankincense, and myrrh.

The wise men were called *magi* or *magicians* in the original language of the Bible. But they didn't pull rabbits out of hats or cast spells. They studied the stars and were a kind of early scientist. They also may have been priests in other religions. It was their special understanding of the stars that brought them to Bethlehem.

The book of Matthew says that the wise men came from the East. That doesn't sound very specific to us, but the writer was probably referring to Persia (around where Iran is now), Mesopotamia (around where Iraq is now), or Arabia. The men may not have all been from the same place. But by the time they reached Jerusalem, they were traveling together.

There are many legends about the wise men that say where they are from, what their names were, and which of them offered what gift. One leader in the early church even said there were fourteen wise men! Today, the three names of wise men that we most often hear are Gaspar, Melchior, and Balthazar. But the legends don't get all of the details the same, and there is no way to know which are right.

How Many Brothers and Sisters Did Jesus Have?

The Gospel of Mark says that Jesus had four brothers: James, Joses (or Joseph), Judas, and Simon (see Mark 6:3). Mark also says that Jesus had sisters, which means he had more than one, though we don't know how many or what their names were.

Even though Mark says Jesus had brothers and sisters, some Christians don't believe that. One group thinks that the words *brother* and *sister* really mean "cousin." Another group thinks that Jesus' earthly father, Joseph, was an older man who was a widower. They think the brothers and sisters were born to Joseph's first wife. But there is no proof that Joseph had been married before, and there is no good reason to think Mark didn't mean to use the words *brother* and *sister*.

Did They Believe in Him?

The answer is yes, no, and maybe. When Jesus was alive, his brothers and sisters did not believe in him. In fact, they thought Jesus was crazy for thinking that he was the Messiah! They even tried to take him away so that people wouldn't listen to him. Of course, that didn't work.

After Jesus was raised from the dead, however, at least two of his brothers believed in him. Judas (also called Jude) wrote one of the books of the New Testament. And the apostle Paul lists Jesus' brother James as one of the witnesses Jesus appeared to after his resurrection. Not only that, but James became the leader of the church in Jerusalem and wrote one of the first books of the New Testament. He believed in Jesus so much that he was killed for preaching the gospel.

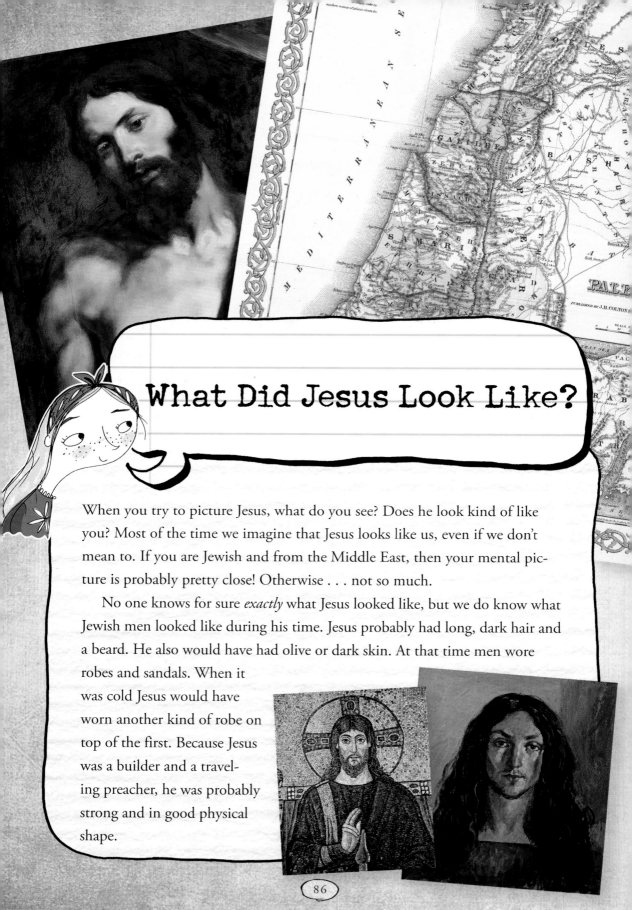

What Did Jesus Look Like?

When you try to picture Jesus, what do you see? Does he look kind of like you? Most of the time we imagine that Jesus looks like us, even if we don't mean to. If you are Jewish and from the Middle East, then your mental picture is probably pretty close! Otherwise . . . not so much.

No one knows for sure *exactly* what Jesus looked like, but we do know what Jewish men looked like during his time. Jesus probably had long, dark hair and a beard. He also would have had olive or dark skin. At that time men wore robes and sandals. When it was cold Jesus would have worn another kind of robe on top of the first. Because Jesus was a builder and a traveling preacher, he was probably strong and in good physical shape.

What Was His House Like?

Jesus was from a poor family in a poor country. His house was probably unlike any house you've seen before. Many Middle Eastern homes back then had three rooms. One room was where the meals were made and where the whole family ate and slept together. It was like having the kitchen, dining room, family room, and all the bedrooms all in one room, except it wasn't very big. Another room was a guest room, and no one stayed there except guests. Many times, the guest room was built on the roof, so sometimes it was called the upper room. The third room was a place where animals were kept. A family might own some goats to use for milk, for example. And there was often a courtyard outside the house, where some of the baking or washing would be done. These houses were usually made of stone, but sometimes they were built on top of a cave so that the cave could be used as the room for the animals. And sometimes the whole house would be in the cave. In Israel, where Jesus was from, some people still lived in caves until the 1900s.

Why Was Jesus Baptized?

John the Baptist preached that the Jews should repent of their sins and that the Messiah was coming soon. When people listened to him, they would repent—feel sorry about and want to turn away from their sins—and he would baptize them, washing them with the water of the Jordan River. Being baptized didn't really wash away anyone's sins. But it was a way for the people to show they were sorry for their sins and that they would try harder to keep God's law.

When Jesus came and asked John to baptize him, he hadn't started his ministry yet. But John knew who he was, and he refused to baptize Jesus.

He didn't feel worthy to baptize the Messiah! He even told Jesus to baptize him.

But Jesus told John to baptize him because it was the right thing to do. Jesus had come to live as a man in every way. By being baptized, he was showing the world he was one of God's people and doing God's work. It was an announcement that he was beginning his ministry.

What Does Salvation Mean?

Salvation means being saved. If you believe in Jesus, you are saved from your sins. Every single thing you do that goes against God's law deserves punishment. And every sin, no matter how small, makes you imperfect. God can't allow anyone who is not perfect to be with him. That means even something you might think is just a "little sin" actually makes you so imperfect that it separates you from God forever.

You can't do anything to get yourself back to God. Jesus is the one who rescues you from your separation from God. He saves you when you believe that he died for your sins and accept his gift of grace. And when you do that, you receive salvation. That means you will live with God forever and never be separated from him.

Why Did Jesus Have Apostles? Who Were They?

Apostles had the same job as prophets did in the Old Testament. They were specially chosen by God to speak his message, and anyone who didn't believe them didn't believe God.

Jesus chose a small group of men that he gave his message to so that they could spread it all over the world after his ministry on earth was finished. Most of these men were disciples, the twelve men who traveled with Jesus and were taught by him. They were Peter, James (son of Zebedee), John, Andrew, Philip, Thomas, Nathanael (Bartholomew), Matthew, James (son of Alphaeus), Thaddaeus, and Simon the Zealot. There was also the disciple named Judas. But after he betrayed Jesus and died, he was replaced by a believer named Matthias.

Jesus also appeared to his brother James, who became the leader of the church in Jerusalem and wrote the book of James. Another of his brothers, Jude, was also an apostle who wrote a book in the New Testament. Lastly, there was Paul, who is the only one who became an apostle after Jesus ascended to heaven.

How Did Jesus Feed 5,000 People at One Time?

Actually, Jesus fed way more than that! At what many people call the "feeding of the 5,000," there were 5,000 *men*. But there were probably also that many women, too! Then you would have to count their children, if any. So the total number would have been way over *10,000* people!

The Bible says that Jesus took five loaves of bread and two fish, prayed over them, then had his disciples pass out the food. They may have put the food into a few baskets, then divided up to go into the crowd and pass it out. They must have felt foolish at first, since it looked like they would run out of food after giving it to the first three or four families. *But it never ran out.*

The food just kept on coming, no matter how much they gave. Not only did the disciples feed the whole crowd, but they had 12 baskets of leftovers—which was way more than they started with!

Of course, this sounds impossible. But since Jesus is God, and he himself created the world from nothing, why should we think feeding a crowd is any harder to do? Jesus didn't even need the two fish or five loaves. He could have simply made food appear in each person's lap. But what matters is that Jesus did it to prove what he said was true and could be trusted.

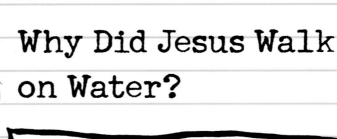

Why Did Jesus Walk on Water?

Jesus wanted to spend some time alone in prayer, so he sent the disciples across the lake to the next place they were going. He told them he would meet them there. The disciples struggled to get across the lake because the water was rough and the wind was strong.

But then, very late at night, not long before dawn, the disciples saw Jesus walking toward them on the water. At first they thought he was a ghost! Then Peter told Jesus to order him to walk on the water too. That would prove that it was really Jesus. So that's what Jesus did.

Peter started out on the water toward Jesus, walking just fine at first. But when he saw the wind, he got scared and started to sink. Jesus caught him and took him to the boat. As soon as he did, the wind stopped.

This may sound like a strange miracle for Jesus to do. But if someone told you that they were God, they would have to prove it to you, right? And one way to do that is by showing that they have control over the natural order of the earth. By walking on water, which is impossible for us to do, Jesus was proving that he is more powerful than the earth, that he rules over it. And when Jesus got in the boat, the disciples worshiped him and confessed he was God. By walking on water, Jesus was showing his disciples his true identity as God.

Is There a Right or Wrong Way to Pray?

One of Jesus' disciples asked this question too! And Jesus told him (and the other disciples) the right way to pray. You may know it as the Lord's Prayer:

> Our Father which art in heaven, Hallowed be thy name.
> Thy kingdom come, Thy will be done in earth,
>   as it is in heaven.
> Give us this day our daily bread.
> And forgive us our debts, as we forgive our
>   debtors.
> And lead us not into temptation, but deliver
>   us from evil: For thine is the kingdom, and
>   the power, and the glory, for ever. Amen.
>
> MATTHEW 6:9-13, KJV

If you've learned the Lord's Prayer, this may be the exact version you know, using older words like *thy* and *thine*, or you may know a different version. But there's nothing magical about the words alone, and simply saying them doesn't mean you are really praying. Praying is something you do with your heart more than with your mouth. But Jesus gave us these words to help us know how our hearts should feel. When we pray, the first thing we should do is honor God and tell him that his ways are better than ours ("hallowed [respected; honored] be thy name . . . thy will be done [may your plans come true]"). This also tells God that we know he is in control of everything. Only after we tell God how much we need him should we ask him to provide for us. If we make prayer just a list of things we want, we're treating God like he is our servant instead of the other way around. God knows everything already, including all the things we need. But by asking him, we are telling God how much we need him. After that, we should ask for forgiveness and for the strength to forgive others. Lastly, we ask for protection from "temptation" (the desire to do things that we shouldn't do) and "evil." In closing, we turn all the glory back to God, as a reminder that it's all his—"the kingdom, and the power, and the glory, for ever."

Jesus also tells us how *not* to pray. He says we should not do it in a way that draws attention to ourselves, trying to look holy to other people.

Why Didn't Jesus Heal Everybody?

First of all, Jesus *did* heal a whole lot of people. In fact, John tells us that if we were to write down all of the things that Jesus did, the *whole world* couldn't contain all the books that would have to be written. Healing people was one of the most amazing things that people saw Jesus do in his ministry. He even brought some people back to life after they had died.

As more and more people heard about what Jesus could do, the crowds that followed him grew larger and larger. Jesus used these opportunities to teach everyone around him. Because he was teaching about God and speaking for God like a prophet, he had to prove that he should be believed. All of those healings were miracles that gave people proof, a reason to believe what Jesus said.

But the work that God sent Jesus to do was not to heal people. If that was what he was sent for, then he wouldn't have needed to preach, and he wouldn't have needed to die on a cross for us. He would have just healed

people. Even though Jesus didn't heal everyone personally, he still gave them what they needed most: the free offer of salvation from their sins. Jesus' work on the cross not only defeated death, but it defeated all the other effects of sin, including sickness. In the new heavens and new earth, those things will not exist.

What Are Parables? Why Did Jesus Tell Them?

A parable is a story that is told to help people understand a lesson. Jesus taught a lot of things that were very hard to understand because they were about God, how he wants us to live, and other things we can't see. Whether he was talking to farmers and fishermen or to rulers and teachers, Jesus told stories to help people understand him.

Can you remember some of Jesus' parables? You probably thought about someone working in a field or walking along a road or about a garden. These are all things that everyone Jesus preached to could understand. They didn't have to have a lot of school or live in a certain place or have an important job to get his message.

Jesus could have used a lot of big words and told us things that we could never understand. It would have made him sound really smart—but it wouldn't have been very helpful for the rest of us, would it? Instead, Jesus told the truth in parables so that everyone back then *and* everyone who has lived since then could understand him.

Who Is the Good Samaritan?

Samaria was the area between Galilee (the area Jesus was from) and Judea (where Jerusalem is). The people who lived there were descendants of Jews who married non-Jews. This made the Jews in Galilee and Judea think of the Samaritans as people who were not really Jewish.

The Samaritans did not worship in Jerusalem; they had their own temple. Even though they had a Bible, it was made up of only the first five books of the Jewish Bible, which were the ones written by Moses. Because the Samaritans rejected all but one of the prophets and didn't worship God the way he'd told them to, the Jews hated them.

The Jews hated Samaritans so much that they did everything they could not to travel through Samaria. They would cross to the east side of the Jordan River when they went between Galilee and Judea just to stay out of Samaria, even though it added several days to their journey.

But Jesus did not hate the Samaritans. Although he usually took the normal roads around the area, sometimes he went the shorter way—through Samaria. He knew that the Samaritans needed his good news just as much as everybody else.

When Jesus told the parable of the Good Samaritan, it shocked his listeners because they would never expect someone they hated so much to be the hero of the story.

Why Didn't Some People Believe in Jesus?

Have you ever thought about how amazing it would have been to be alive when Jesus was alive? We picture it every time we read about him in Scripture. But what is hard to imagine is that most of the people Jesus preached to didn't believe in him. Even most of those who saw him perform miracles and healings didn't believe. Why is that? What did those people not see or understand?

Some people who do not believe would rather trust in themselves for salvation. Although Jesus graciously offers the free gift of salvation, no other religion or way of living offers eternal life as a free gift. Every other religion makes salvation something that you earn. People who did not believe in Jesus then—and people who do not believe in Jesus now—believe they can earn their own salvation. Some people think they will be saved by keeping the laws and rules of a different religion. For some, it is by doing more good things in their life than bad things. Trusting in Jesus would mean admitting that they need Jesus to do it for them. For most of us, admitting we can't do something important is humiliating or even shameful. Jesus came to rescue people from that. But those who don't want to admit they can't earn their own salvation choose themselves over Jesus.

Who Were the High Priests?

The ceremonies in the Tabernacle and Temple could not be performed by just anyone. God said that only Moses' brother, Aaron, along with his sons, could be the priests who carried out the sacrifices and duties. Aaron was the first high priest, or chief priest. It was his job to enter the Most Holy Place once a year and sprinkle blood onto the top of the Ark of the Covenant. When Aaron died, one of his sons became high priest, and the priesthood was only passed down to his descendants. The high priest was also head of a group of seventy religious leaders, called the Sanhedrin, that was a kind of court that made sure people followed the law. It was the Sanhedrin who arrested Jesus and found him guilty of blasphemy, which had to be punished by death.

Who Was Pilate?

The Romans ruled the area where Jesus lived, and they put a ruler there to be the governor (called a prefect). The prefect when Jesus was crucified was named Pontius Pilate. There are several legends about Pilate and what happened to him after Jesus was executed, but except for the trial of Jesus, we don't know much about him. He had a reputation for being cruel. When he first became prefect he made the Jews mad on purpose by carrying banners with images of Tiberius Caesar into Jerusalem. The Jews thought that pictures of people were too much like idols, so they got very upset. Pilate threatened to kill all the protesters, but then he took the pictures down when Tiberius told him to. He also stole money from the Temple treasury to build an aqueduct, then killed anyone who protested. Even though the Romans ruled Judea, they let the Jews govern themselves in most ways. But the Sanhedrin could not put people to death. They had to get Rome to do that. So when the high priest found Jesus guilty of blasphemy and wanted to kill him, the Sanhedrin had to send him before Pilate and try to convince him to put Jesus to death. Pilate didn't think Jesus had done anything wrong, but he didn't want the Jews to report to Caesar that Pilate had refused to kill a person claiming to be King of the Jews. Pilate chose to have Jesus killed, but he washed his hands when he made the judgment to show that he was not responsible for Jesus' death. Eventually Pilate's cruelty became too much even for the Romans, and he was fired as prefect for his treatment of Samaritan rebels a few years after Jesus died.

Where Was the Cross?

The place where Jesus was killed was called Golgotha, which means "Place of the Skull" in Aramaic. It is also called Calvary, which is the Latin word that means the same thing. Golgotha was outside Jerusalem but near the city. The spot was probably known to everyone who lived there and many who visited because the crucified bodies were meant to be seen easily, as a warning not to fight against the Romans.

There are two places that claim to be Golgotha that can be visited today. One of them still looks a lot like it probably did in Jesus' time. It's near a small cliff that even kind of looks like a skull. But people didn't think it might be Golgotha until the middle of the 1800s. The other place is in the middle of the Old City walls of Jerusalem, inside the Church of the Holy Sepulchre. Bible teachers used to say this couldn't be the place because it was not outside the city walls. But archaeologists have found that the wall around the city didn't go around that part of the city when Jesus died. As Jerusalem grew, a new wall had to be built, and that is when the church was brought into the city. This is the spot that the first Christians remembered as Golgotha.

Why Wasn't Jesus' Dad There?

When Jesus was crucified, his mother, Mary, was there, but the Bible doesn't say anything about Joseph being there. Because it was Passover, Joseph would have been required to be at the feast, just like any other Jewish man. The only exceptions were made for people who could not travel. The walk from Nazareth to Jerusalem was about ninety miles and could take five or six days. Joseph may have been too weak to make the trip because he was sick or injured. But it's more likely that Joseph had died by the time Jesus began his ministry.

The last time Joseph is mentioned in the Bible is when Jesus visited the Temple during Passover when he was twelve. When Jesus' family came to try to talk to him while he was teaching in Capernaum, the Bible mentions his mother and brothers, but not Joseph. True, he may have stayed home to work. But since the family thought Jesus was crazy and had come to take him home, Joseph—the father and head of the family—would probably have been there if he were still alive.

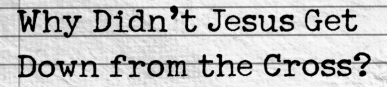

Why Didn't Jesus Get Down from the Cross?

Crucifixion was the worst kind of punishment the Romans could give. It was extremely cruel and painful, and it took a long time. It was also humiliating because it was done where the most people possible could see it happen.

For Jesus it was even worse because he was innocent. He was not a criminal, and he didn't deserve to die. He hadn't done anything wrong in his whole life! And because he was God, he could have taken himself off the cross. He could have kept his enemies from ever catching him to begin with! When Peter tried

to fight for Jesus when he was arrested, Jesus told him that he could call on an army of angels to protect him. He had the power to escape the cross and the power to come down from it, yet he didn't.

He didn't because the whole reason Jesus came to earth was to die on that cross. He didn't come just to teach and heal and be a good example to people. He came to pay for the sins of everyone who would believe in him. And he paid for them on the cross. If Jesus had gotten off the cross, our sins would not be paid for, and we would have no hope of salvation. But God loves you so much that he sent his Son, Jesus, to die a death he did not deserve so that you could live forever with God.

113

Where Was Jesus While He Was Dead?

When Jesus was dying on the cross, one of the thieves who was crucified next to him became a believer. Jesus told the thief that he would be in paradise with Jesus that very day. Paradise is the place where people who are forgiven go when they die while they wait for the Last Judgment and the new heaven and new earth. It is being with God, enjoying his presence. So during the time before the Resurrection, while Jesus' body was dead, he was in heaven with God the Father.

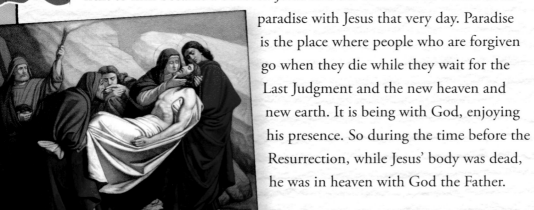

Where Is Jesus Now?

Jesus is in heaven and sits at the right hand of the Father. He still has his human body, although it no longer can die or get sick or get old. But because he is God, he is also present everywhere.

What Happened to Jesus' Tomb?

The Gospel of John says that there was a garden where Jesus was crucified, and that it was used for burying people. It was probably a rocky area where stones had been cut to build the Temple. When it wasn't used for that, it was used for burials. The tombs were cut into the rock walls, and bodies were put inside.

When Jesus was buried, everyone knew where his tomb was—his followers, as well as the Jewish authorities and the Romans. The tomb was guarded and watched by soldiers. A hundred years later, when the Jews rebelled against the Romans, the Roman emperor Hadrian tried to take away all the places that were important to Jews and Christians. He built a temple to the Roman god Jupiter where the Jewish Temple used to stand. He also knew where the tomb that people remembered as Jesus' was. He filled it in with dirt, and then built a temple to the Roman goddess Venus on top of it. Two hundred years later, Helena, the mother of the emperor Constantine, visited the Holy Land and tried to find Jesus' tomb, as well as other places important to Christians. The people of Jerusalem knew that the temple of Venus stood above the tomb—instead of erasing the place where Jesus was buried, Hadrian had marked it! Helena had the temple to Venus torn down, and the tomb was discovered. Constantine built a small chapel around it, and other people added on to it, eventually making the building called the Church of the Holy Sepulchre. The church has been damaged by fires and earthquakes, and the tomb has been damaged and rebuilt several times. But this is probably the location of the actual tomb.

Who Is the Holy Spirit?

The Bible says that there is only one God. But it also calls Jesus *God*, and Jesus prays to the Father, who is God. The Holy Spirit is also God. While all three—Father, Son, and Holy Spirit—are fully God, there is still only one God. That means that each of the three is a person, not a thing. God is three persons, but only one God.

Confusing? Yes. But remember: there is only one God, and he is totally different from anything else that exists. There is nothing to compare him to. Each person of God is not just a part of God, but each one is completely God. There is nothing that one person has that another does not.

In Acts, Jesus spoke of the Holy Spirit as a gift that the disciples would receive. He said that they would be baptized in the Holy Spirit just as John baptized people in water. We see that power in Acts 2, during the day of Pentecost. When the Holy Spirit arrived, suddenly the disciples could speak in all different languages so that they could share the gospel with everyone around them. This was because of the gift—the power—of the Holy Spirit that Jesus had sent to guide his disciples. That same gift and power is still available to us all.

How Does the Holy Spirit Live in Me?

When the Holy Spirit begins to live in your heart, you are born again. The Holy Spirit then teaches you to live differently than you did before. You will want to do things that please God and live like Jesus lived. That doesn't mean you stop sinning. That will only happen when you are in heaven with God. But it does mean that you will begin a lifelong journey of learning and changing to be more like Jesus.

And it is the Holy Spirit who helps you through it all. Sometimes he helps you in a way that is almost like talking to you. Sometimes the Holy Spirit tells you to do or choose one thing over another. The Holy Spirit can even change how you see and think about things. He is like a special pair of glasses that changes how you see the world.

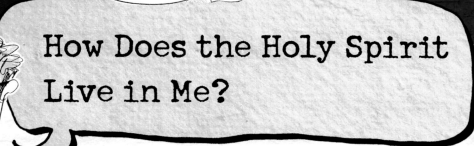

When Is Jesus Coming Back?

While Jesus was on earth, he told his disciples several times that he would return to judge everyone who ever lived. When he comes back, it will be the end of this world. Those who believe in Jesus will live with God forever.

Ever since Jesus died, there have been people who have tried to figure out when he will come back. Some people thought it would be before the last apostle died. Some people thought it would be on New Year's Day of the year 1000 or 2000. Some people have used other ways to pick a certain day, month, and year.

But the truth is that no one knows. Jesus even told his disciples that no one can know the time. Knowing *when* it will happen is not as important as knowing it *will* happen. We need to live in a way that honors God, no matter when he comes back for us.

What Is Heaven Like?

Although God is everywhere, heaven is a special place where he is worshiped and from where he rules. It is so different from anything we have ever seen that it is hard to imagine. Jesus took the apostle John there to show him things that hadn't happened yet. Then John wrote down what he had seen, as best he could.

John said that heaven has a throne surrounded by a rainbow, and the throne rumbles like thunder and flashes like lightning. Seven torches that burn with the Spirit of God stand before the throne on a floor that is like a sea of glass. A golden altar sits before the throne, and smoke from incense rises from it.

Everyone who believed in God before they died is in heaven. Heaven also has many creatures that we have never seen. More angels than we could ever count surround the throne. Twenty-four elders sit on smaller thrones around the main throne. And there are four creatures who have six wings, are covered with eyes, and have faces like a lion, an ox, a human, or an eagle. Everyone there worships God perfectly.

Nothing will ever die, you will never be sad, you'll never cry, and you will never get hurt. You'll never be sick or get hungry, and you'll never want anything you don't have. God will provide everything you ever want and need. But what you will want and need more than anything is him.

What Are the "New Heaven and New Earth"?

The way the world is now is not like it was when God created it. When sin entered the world through the disobedience of Adam, it affected all of creation. The whole world and everything in it suffers from the curse of sin. Sometimes we think of Jesus' death on the cross as the way that people are saved. But because Jesus died for sin, he also breaks the curse that is on the earth.

When Jesus comes back to judge the world, he will create a new heaven and a new earth. And like our own bodies, they will never be hurt by sin—because there will be no sin. The new heaven and new earth is the place where everyone who believes in Jesus will spend eternity living with God. Jesus showed his apostle John a vision of it, and John wrote it down in the book of Revelation. Even though John describes a place incredibly beautiful and perfect, his words probably don't even come close to telling just how wonderful it is.

Acknowledgments

There are so many people who pour their lives into the making of a book.

From our families, who tolerate our frenzied deadlines (well, Amy's—I don't think Doug has ever been in a frenzy about anything), to the person at the printer watching warm signatures roll off the line. We are so thankful for every single person who has been a part of the making of this book.

To name a few, Amy's family: Daniel, Michael, and Ethan for their continued help and encouragement, and to Indiana Jones Parker, the puppy who has made sure I've had my daily walk, despite those frenzied deadlines. And always, to my parents and grandparents for giving me the foundation on which I daily build my faith.

Doug's family: Jennifer, Julian, Mia, Connolly, Trey, and Neely, who voluntarily (and involuntarily) had many of the answers in the book practiced on them.

To Dan Lynch, Bob Starnes, and Brock Starnes of Brentwood Studios: thank you for being a team of the highest caliber, as well as trusted mentors and friends in this publishing journey.

To the fine folks at Tyndale, who make excellence the standard, including Linda Howard, who entertained this idea from the beginning, and Sarah Rubio, our unicorn of an editor, who has made the process of perfecting this manuscript painless and even—dare I say it?—fun! And to everyone else there whom we've never met yet who have been cheering us on from behind the scenes: thank you.

Lastly and mostly, to God from whom all blessings flow: thank you for making this possible, for giving us the words and the outlet and the capacity to learn more about you and to then be able to share what we've learned. All power and glory is yours in spite of our weaknesses.

Thank you all. We hope we make you proud.

Amy & *Doug*

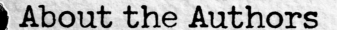

About the Authors

Doug Powell is a Christian apologist, author, graphic designer, programmer, and recording artist. He has appeared on *Late Night with Conan O'Brien*, CNN, NPR, *World Cafe*, *Prime Time America*, *White Horse Inn*, *Stand to Reason*, and *SoundRezn*. He is the author, designer, and programmer of the iWitness series of books and apps, and author/designer of the bestselling book the *Holman QuickSource Guide to Christian Apologetics*. He is also a contributor to *The Apologetics Study Bible* and the *Apologetics Study Bible for Students*. Doug holds a master's degree in apologetics from Biola University.

Amy Parker has written more than fifty books for children, teens, and adults, with over 1.5 million copies sold. She has collaborated with authors ranging from *New York Times* bestsellers to her very own son. Two of these collaborations—*Firebird* and *Courageous Teens*—are recipients of *Christian Retailing*'s Best Awards. But Amy's greatest reward is being a wife to Daniel and a mom to their amazing sons, Michael and Ethan.

Got more questions about the Bible?

Send them to us at

Bigbiblequestions@tyndale.com

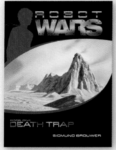

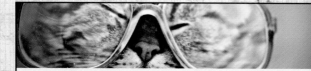

FOR ADVENTURERS

The Wormling series

Red Rock Mysteries series

FOR COMEDIANS

The Dead Sea Squirrels series

FOR ARTISTS

Made to Create with All My
Heart and Soul

Be Bold

FOR ANIMAL LOVERS

Winnie the Horse Gentler series

Starlight Animal Rescue series

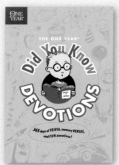

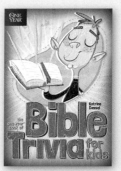